before the communist revolution Russian history through 1919

by Stuart A. Kallen

Consultant: Margaret Robinson Preska, Ph.D. Russian History
President, Mankato State University [1979-1992]

Published by Abdo & Daughters, 6535 Cecilia Circle, Edina, Minnesota 55439.

Copyright © 1992 by Abdo Consulting Group, Inc., Pentagon Tower, P.O. Box 36036, Minneapolis, Minnesota 55435. International copyrights reserved in all counties. No part of this book may be reproduced in any form without written permission from the publisher. Printed in the United States.

Photo credits: Archive Photos-10, 13, 23, 27, 30, 33, 35, 47, 50
                   FPG International-cover, 4, 14, 41, 42, 45

Edited by: Rosemary Wallner

Library of Congress Cataloging-in-Publication Data

Kallen, Stuart A., 1955-
        Before the communist revolution / written by Stuart A. Kallen ; [edited by Rosemary Wallner].
             p. cm. — (The Rise & fall of the Soviet Union)
        Includes index.
        Summary: Surveys the early years of Russian history, from 500 A.D. to the revolution that
placed the Communist Party in power.
        ISBN 1-56239-100-3 (lib. bdg.)
        1. Soviet Union—History—Juvenile literature. [1. Soviet Union—History.] I. Wallner,
Rosemary, 1964- . II. Title. III. Series: Kallen, Stuart A., 1955- Rise & fall of the Soviet Union.
        DK246.K35 1992
        947—dc20
                                                                              92-13472
                                                                                 CIP
                                                                                  AC

table of contents

Page

5   the wall comes tumbling down

9   marauding conquerors

12   vladimir's onion-domes

17   ivans of the north

21   peter the great giant

26   catherine the great

29   invasions, terrorists, and revolutions

32   setting free the serfs

36   the road to revolution

38   the bomb throwers

40   bloody nicholas

46   the roots of communism

49   world war I

51   rasputin's last gasp

52   the falling czar

53   the communists seize power

55   final word

57   glossary

58   index

the wall comes tumbling down

"Clink, clank, clink." The steadfast rhythm of a thousand unwavering hammers pounded on concrete. "Clink, clank, clink." The noise changed pitch as others joined in with pipes, crowbars, and anything else that was sturdy enough to attack the ten-foot obstacle. A crowd too large to measure had gathered at the Berlin Wall in Germany as it was being torn down, chip by chip. The masses cheered as the separate chips of wall turned to huge piles of dust. Finally, a whole section of the wall came tumbling down. Ten thousand camera bulbs flashed blue-white as people from the divided Germanys swarmed together, united again after twenty-eight years. The eyes of the world squinted into the camera's glow. They were watching history being made.

First one, then dozens of people climbed up on the Wall. Seconds later, a tidal wave of humanity engulfed the Wall and it disappeared beneath an ocean of bodies. The people danced, blew horns, played guitars, and beat drums. Champagne corks popped where, only the week before, soldiers would have shot the partiers to death. Now, ten-thousand dancing feet stomped into sand the Berlin Wall, which for thirty years had imprisoned the people of East Germany.

The cracks that split the Berlin Wall on that day, November 9, 1989, were felt far beyond Germany. Once those cracks were started, they became fissures and finally canyons that ripped apart the Communist government in the Soviet Union, the largest country on Earth.

For it was the Soviets, not the Germans who had built the Berlin Wall in 1961 in order to keep East German people from moving away from East Germany. For twenty-eight years, the Wall had stood as a symbol of a divided Europe and of the Communist suppression of freedom. When the Soviet Union built the Wall, it became one of the only governments in the history of the world that had to build a wall to keep people from leaving their rule.

The Wall was surrounded by land mines, trained killer wolfhounds, and soldiers who had orders to shoot to kill. And kill they did. During the lifetime of the Berlin Wall, 5,000 East Germans attempted to cross the wall; 191 people died trying. Another 5,000 desperately tunneled, blasted, flew, or drove their way to freedom. The last person was shot to death trying to climb over the Berlin Wall in May 1989.

East Germany was not the first or only country that took their orders from Moscow, the capital of the Soviet Union. The governments of Poland, Hungary, Yugoslavia, Romania, Bulgaria, and Czechoslovakia, were all "satellite" governments of the Soviet Union. If the people tried to protest Moscow's iron rule, as had happened in Czechoslovakia in 1968, Soviet tanks thundered through the streets, shooting and gassing any protesters in their way. The rulers in Moscow had a long and bloody history of swallowing up smaller neighboring countries.

But when the Berlin Wall fell, the Soviet Army did not try to stop it, as they would have only one year before. The talk of freedom which had been whispered about in secret for forty years, had turned into such a deafening shout that it had overwhelmed the Soviet system and dissolved it to dust, much like the Berlin Wall.

Overnight, men who had been imprisoned for speaking out against Soviet rule became national leaders in Czechoslovakia and elsewhere. Meanwhile, powerful Soviet generals slunk off alone, into the night. How could all this happen against such incredible odds? How could the largest country on Earth, with the second most powerful army, suddenly give up their system of government?

To answer these questions, we must go back in history, to a distant time and place. Back five hundred years or more, to a place of intrigue and violence, starvation and revolutions. Back to the early years of Soviet history, when the Soviet Union was called Russia, and the fertile land beckoned many invading armies.

marauding conquerors

The country of Russia has been invaded by a who's who of world famous conquerors. From Attila the Hun to Napoleon and Adolf Hitler, almost every power-mad leader in history has taken a shot at conquering Russia. Some men succeeded, many failed.

Ancient marauding clans like the Khazars, the Avars, and the Goths surged across Russia's grassy steppes. Each tribe managed to rule the lands and the people until another more powerful tribe vanquished them. The infamous Attila the Hun, from north-central Asia, conquered Russia and then went on to terrorize much of Europe, rampaging as far west as France. The feared and hated Attila was a terrorist who murdered his own brother to gain power. The Huns captured people to use as slaves. Some slaves were sold to the Romans, many were tortured and killed.

Attila the Hun conquered Russia and then went on to terrorize much of Europe.

In the meantime, a group of farmers and trappers known as the Slavs (the word "slave" comes from the word "Slav") settled in the forested areas near present-day Kiev and Moscow. While fierce Mongolian horsemen and nomadic Khazars came and went, the Slavs settled in and became the first true Russians. The Slavs also spread westward into Europe to become the distant relatives of today's Yugoslavians, Czechoslovakians, Poles, and Bulgarians.

The exact origins of the name "Russia" are unclear, but some historians believe that the name was a gift from Viking traders who came from present-day Scandinavia. The traders floated their ships down the Volkov and Dnieper rivers in the ninth century. They were traveling through the Slavic heartland to the rich markets of Byzantium, which included parts of present-day Egypt, Syria, and Greece. In time, a group of Viking tradesmen, known as the "Rus" established trading posts in the Slavs' territory. Two of the trading posts, Kiev and Novgorod grew into fortified cities ruled by Norse princes. By A.D. 882, Kiev had grown into a thriving state that had become the ancestral home to modern Russia.

vladimir's onion-domes

n the year A.D. 980, Russia came under the rule of Vladimir I, the first in a long series of iron-fisted rulers who used force to shape Russian history. By this time in history, many parts of the world had adopted a major religion. Christians governed Europe, Muslims the Arab world , and Jews parts of southern Russia. Vladimir decided that a religion would help bring his country together in unity. He decided to impose one religion on all the different pagan cults that were practicing in Russia. But which one? He sent his messengers to gather information on Islam, Judaism, and Christianity.

Vladimir rejected Islam because it forbade drinking alcohol. "Drinking," he said, "is the joy of the Russes." Next, Vladimir rejected Judaism because its people had had to flee their original homeland and he did not want to adopt the religion of a dispersed people. That left Christianity, but Vladimir "found no glory" in the Roman Catholic Church.

Vladimir I was the first of many iron-fisted rulers who used forced to shape Russian history.

Onion-domed buildings in Russia reflect Vladimir's
interest in the Greek orthodox religion.

However, a branch of the Catholic Church, the Greek Eastern Orthodox, dazzled Vladimir with its gold onion-domed churches. After visiting one of the churches, Vladimir stated, "The Greeks led us to the buildings where they worshiped their god, and we did not know whether we were in heaven or on earth, for on earth there is no such splendor or beauty." Vladimir was baptized in the Orthodox church and forced all his subjects to do the same.

Today, one of the most recognizable symbols of the Soviet Union is St. Basil's Cathedral in Moscow. The church, which serves as a backdrop for almost every television newscast, has nine onion-domed chapels built in the Greek and Russian Orthodox style. The church was finished in 1555.

The unity that Vladimir had hoped to achieve was not to last. That is because Russia had two separate societies. While the rich enjoyed abundant and happy lives, the bulk of Russian people were poor beyond imagining. The upper classes, called boyars, feasted on the finest food served on plates of silver and gold. They wore expensive clothes and were entertained by minstrels, poets, and artists. In contrast the peasants, called serfs, were tied to the land like slaves.

They worked from sunup to sundown in order to support the boyars. The serfs lived in squalid shacks and knew only wretchedness, hunger, and disease. The extremely long and frigid Russian winters intensified the suffering of the serfs.

Kiev fell to the Mongolian Tarters in the thirteenth century. The Tartars moved out of northern Asia and swept across Russia, first looting, then putting the torch to Russia's towns and cities. At the time, the fierce arrow-shooting Mongolian horsemen were the most powerful army in the world. They rounded up thousands of people and sold them into slavery. The Mongolian Tarters, known as the Golden Horde, seized women, children, and old men to use as shields against advancing armies. After a successful battle, the Mongols celebrated by laying boards over their captured prisoners. They danced and feasted upon the boards as their prisoners suffocated below.

Two centuries of Mongolian oppression isolated Russia from the cultural advances that were taking place in the rest of Europe. Industry and arts had no chance to develop during this time of torture and looting.

However, the art of warfare, some Mongolian language, the idea of royalty, and colorful clothing styles became ingrained in the Russian culture.

ivans of the north

In the late thirteenth century, the northern Slavs became known as the Muscovy people who lived in a little wooden town called Moscow. The Muscovy were loosely controlled by the Golden Horde, but eventually the Mongolian Tarters brought their own downfall by fighting among themselves. The little town of Moscow soon became the spiritual capital of Russia by accident — the head of the Russian Church was visiting Moscow when he died. The Moscow princes persuaded the next church head to move the church headquarters to Moscow. Thus fortified, the Moscow princes threw off the yoke of Tartar rule in 1380.

By 1462, a potent ruler named Ivan III united Russia under his rule. He called himself the Czar, or Tsar, which is Russian for "Caesar." This was the title of the ancient emperors of Rome. His court called him Ivan the Great.

Ivan the Great was an evenhanded ruler who did many things to advance Russian culture. That cannot be said about his grandson, Ivan IV, who took over the throne when Ivan the Great died. Ivan IV became known as "Ivan the Terrible." Ivan was not born terrible, he became that way from watching violent palace intrigue. When Ivan was three years old his father died. When he was eight, his mother died mysteriously, probably by poisoning. Two noble families seized power and denied Ivan food, water, and clothing while they ransacked the imperial treasury. Murder, execution, and larceny were the order of the day, and unspeakable crimes were committed before the eyes of the future Russian king.

At the age of thirteen, Ivan IV donned the official robes of the czar. During his first days as king, he had an advisor, whom he disliked, clubbed to death by palace dog keepers. Ivan's power was never doubted after that incident.

At sixteen, Ivan was crowned at an official public ceremony. He was showered with gold and silver as bells rang throughout the kingdom. Three weeks later, he married Anastasia Zakharina-Romanov, a member of a royal family that would play a central role in Russian history. Anastasia was beautiful and intelligent, and for a while, Ivan was not so terrible.

During Ivan IV's happy years with Anastasia, he brought scholars, artists, and craftsmen from the West to bring Russia up to date with the rest of Europe. He opened a trade route with England and improved diplomatic relations with more powerful countries. Ivan's army expanded Russia's borders to include Siberia, Lithuania, and Poland. Unfortunately, support for the expansionist armies caused the serfs' condition to decline further. Ivan restricted movement and forbade travel among the serfs.

In 1560, Anastasia died under suspicious circumstances and the really terrible part of Ivan's reign began. His mind shattered as he ordered the execution of anyone he suspected as being disloyal. The serfs rebelled in the town of Novgorod, so Ivan ordered the town burned to the ground and thousands of serfs put to death.

Ivan then established one of the world's first secret police forces, called the oprichnina. Dressed in black and riding coal-black horses, this band of men, numbering 6,000, rode the countryside. They killed anyone who spoke out against Ivan's terrible reign. Ivan was also the first Russian leader to send his enemies to the newly conquered frozen wastelands of Siberia. When Ivan personally tortured his enemies, he was said to foam at the mouth like a mad dog.

By 1584, Ivan became obsessed with knowing when he would die. He sent for sixty witches from Lapland to predict the specific date of his death. Ivan IV would die, the witches said, on March 18 of that year. On March 17, Ivan the Terrible dropped dead.

peter the great giant

After Ivan's death, the country was swept up in chaos. The period was known as the "Time of Troubles." Poland captured Moscow and burned it to the ground. Pretenders claimed to be Ivan IV's dead grandson and heir to the throne. Eventually, the government was stabilized by Mikhail Romanov, relative of Ivan the Terrible's wife, Anastasia.

At the close of the seventeenth century, the architect of modern Russia, Peter the Great, became the czar. Like Ivan the Terrible, Peter the Great suffered childhood traumas inside the palace. But Peter was able to escape palace intrigue and spent the better part of his childhood roaming the countryside by himself. He helped peasants work, and became a skilled craftsman. People said that he could build houses, cobble shoes, pull teeth, build boats, and cast metal.

When Peter took over the throne at the age of twenty-four, he was almost seven feet tall. His strength was legendary, some said he could bend silver plates with his bare hands.

His appetite for food and drink was extraordinary, and he preferred to indulge in the company of the English, Scottish, Swiss, and Dutch craftsmen who were his friends.

Peter decided that to bring Russia into the modern age, he would travel Europe incognito (in disguise) and learn the ways of Western civilization. He began his journey in 1697, disguised as "Peter the Seaman." Because of his great height and his 270 personal attendants his disguise fooled no one. Peter's journey lasted for eighteen months and took him to Germany and Holland, where he earned a boat builder's certificate. He studied anatomy, surgery, art, and government. The English government lodged Peter in a noble's house where he drunkenly broke the furniture and used portraits for target practice. While Peter was away from Russia, a palace revolt took place there. Peter returned home and had the traitors roasted alive on a spit, one by one. Peter personally oversaw the torture of the revolutionaries.

For all his barbaric behavior, Peter believed Russia should be modernized. He ordered men to shave their beards or else pay a tax. Peter even assisted in the shaving of some noblemen.

Peter the Great, Emperor of Russia, 1672-1725.

Men were to shed their long coats and women their veils. Peter insisted that the nobility dress in the extravagant styles that were popular in France. He also built schools for navigation, mathematics, medicine, philosophy, geography, and politics. He started the first Russian newspaper, printed 600 new book titles, and built a theater on Red Square in Moscow. Peter also modernized and expanded the army, ordering soldiers to melt down church bells and make them into cannons.

Peter the Great decided to build a great city as a monument to himself. The city, to be called St. Petersburg, was designed with the help of Italian and French architects. Tens of thousands of peasants, prisoners of war, and army recruits were forced into labor. Those without shovels were commanded to dig with their hands. They were fed stale bread and drank stagnant marsh water. So many died building the city's 34,000 buildings in nine years, that St. Petersburg is said to be built on bones. Peter the Great made St. Petersburg the Russian capital. Allowing for Peter's warped sense of humor, his palace had "surprise" fountains that sprayed unwary visitors who happened to step on a particular stone.

Another one of Peter the Great's contributions to modern Russia was the reforming of the civil service. He set fourteen grades that civil servants could aspire to. Even peasants could rise out of poverty. Every civil servant above grade eleven could own property, above the eighth grade they could pass the property to their children. This system affected the twentieth-century revolutionary, Lenin, who climbed his way up to the fourth grade, making him technically an aristocrat.

Peter killed his only son and heir to the throne, because he suspected him of disloyalty. Seven years later, Peter the Great jumped into an icy river to save some drowning boatmen. He died of pneumonia several days later.

catherine the great

Peter's modernization created a great rift in Russian society. On one side were the Western-oriented aristocrats. On the other side were the peasants and clergy who violently resisted change from their traditional ways. Less than fifty years later, in 1762, Catherine the Great became another Russian leader to widen this chasm.

Catherine was actually a German whose real name was Sophie. She inherited the Russian throne because Peter the Great had named no successor. Peter's sister, Elizabeth, took the throne, then gave it to her nephew, a German prince named Peter of Holstein. Elizabeth selected Sophie, a minor German princess, to be Peter of Holstein's wife. Sophie adopted the name Catherine and learned the Russian language. Catherine basically ignored her alcoholic husband until she had him killed in a drunken brawl. Catherine then became the Queen of Russia.

Catherine the Great became the Queen of Russia in 1762.

Catherine was highly intelligent and hard working. She rose at five o'clock each morning and spent ten to fifteen hours a day on state papers and legislation. She had an unending appetite for suitors, and rewarded her favorites handsomely. She made one of her boyfriends the King of Poland. For her coronation, Catherine ordered a crown with 5,000 diamonds and 76 matched pearls, set in 399 carats of gold. It was so heavy that Catherine complained that it gave her a headache. She collected 4,000 painting from all over Europe and turned St. Petersburg into one of the most beautiful cities in Europe.

During Catherine's reign, half the population of Russia were serfs, laboring under conditions not much different than slavery. One noblewoman in Catherine's court kept her hairdresser, who was a serf, in a cage so that he would not tell anyone she was bald. As so often before in Russian history, wars raged on various borders and rebellions were staged in many distant towns. Catherine's extravagant tastes further divided and impoverished the country by the time of her death in 1796.

invasions, terrorists, and revolutions

Catherine's son Paul became the next czar of Russia. This weak and ineffectual leader was known as the "Mad Czar" because he kept the dead bodies of his mother and his father, Peter of Holstein, displayed in a cathedral long after their deaths. He also dug up the bodies of his dead enemies and defiled them. Paul was succeeded by Alexander I in 1801.

In 1812, Napoleon, the French general, invaded Russia with 640,000 soldiers. Napoleon had already conquered Italy, Germany, and Spain. After many fierce battles, Napoleon captured Moscow. But his already weakened army soon fell prey to Russia's most powerful secret weapon — the unbearably frigid Russian winter. When Napoleon decided to retreat from Moscow, his starving, frostbitten soldiers died by the thousands. Of the 100,000 soldiers that had left Moscow for France, only 9,000 lived to tell about it.

Alexander I succeeded the "Mad Czar" in 1801

The defeat of Napoleon, who claimed he could conquer the world, left the Russians with added power in the rest of the world. But liberal members of the Russian army decided to demonstrate in St. Petersburg for financial reforms, a constitution, and an end to serfdom. The leaders of the so-called "Decembrist Revolt" were hanged, but their ideas could not be quashed. Between 1825 and 1855, over five hundred revolts took place in the Russian countryside. Terrorism, assassination, and revolution swept the country as Russian progress, once again, fell behind the rest of the major powers in Europe.

setting free the serfs

lexander II became the czar of Russia in 1855. He quickly realized that the government was collapsing. Alexander knew drastic changes were needed to save Russia. He could no longer deny the fact that many people besides the serfs were demanding social justice and government reforms. Almost everyone was against serfdom, so Alexander decided to abolish it.

In 1861, four years before the United States abolished slavery, Alexander freed the serfs. Landowners were very unhappy and did not want to give up their land. Because most serfs only knew how to work the land, not run farms, they would have to be freed slowly. Alexander set up a plan whereby serfs would buy their own land gradually, over the course of several years. The land would be owned by a village commune that would manage the land and collect taxes on it. Serfs could also travel with a passport.

Alexander II freed the Russian serfs in 1861, four years
before the United States abolished slavery.

Many serfs left the land to learn a trade or go into business. The serfs who stayed found that, many times, the communes managed the land poorly. When crops failed, payments could not be made. Food shortages caused by the change sparked riots. Some serfs burned farm property and murdered the landowners.

Alexander instituted other reforms, setting up a banking system, building railroads, and setting up a courts system with judges and juries. Factories sprang up and merchants started stores. For the first time, a Russian could become middle-class without having to inherit money and land. Many people learned to read and write. Education and public health were improved.

Unfortunately, many people were still unhappy with Alexander's reforms. Some revolutionaries wanted socialism for the country. Others wanted a constitution similar to the United States. Others tried to get the peasants to revolt. It seems Alexander's changes created more conflict than they solved.

A Russian peasant, a common sight in rural Russia.

the road to revolution

During the first thousand years of Russian history, there was rarely a time when a war was not being fought somewhere to expand Russian territories. Russia's borders were constantly being disputed as wars were fought with Sweden, Poland, Britain, France, China, and Turkey. The cost of these wars was borne mainly by the serfs whose hard lives were made even harder by food shortages, forced labor, and forced service in the army.

While these external conflicts raged, rifts within Russian society often created chaos. Trusted advisors led palace revolts, queens poisoned kings, kings killed princes, peasants revolted, secret police spied — no one, inside or outside of the government, seemed safe from treachery, deceit, and murder. It should be noted that events like these shaped history in many other countries. But these events happened in Russia with a frequency and intensity known nowhere else.

Because of its unique history, Russia was ripe for a new kind of government. But hobbled with her violent history, putting this new experiment in place would be the hardest thing Russia ever did. In the end, it would prove to be a failure.

the bomb throwers

Terrorist organizations formed in Russia during the rule of Alexander II. One secret organization was known as the Nihilists, who set out to create a new order. Their favorite method of operation was to throw bombs at government officials and buildings. They thought the confusion would cause people to stop following the laws.

One group of Nihilists tried to murder Alexander II several times, once in Paris. In 1881, Alexander was riding in a carriage when a bomb exploded in its path, killing the horses and driver. As Alexander fled, another bomb exploded, blowing him to bits. The assassination was blamed on Russia's Jews. Within weeks, in over 215 towns, mobs ran rampant through the streets of Jewish districts destroying homes and killing thousands of Jewish people. The military and police watched from the sidelines.

The man who had done the most to reform Russia could not do it fast enough to please everyone. Terrorism continued and assassinations were carried out with frightening frequency.

bloody nicholas

lexander III succeeded his father and rolled back many of his reforms. Censorship and landowner powers were returned as the serfs continued to suffer. In 1894, Alexander III died. His son, twenty-six-year-old Nicholas II, took the throne to become the last czar of Russia. He was the last of the Romanov rulers, a line started in 1560 by Ivan the Terrible's wife, Anastasia Romanov. Like the other czars of Russia, he had a nickname — Bloody Nicholas — because his reign was marked with intense violence, bloodshed, riots, revolts, and wars.

Nicholas was a shy, slow-witted, family man. Hardly the type of man needed to rule Russia during this time of upheaval. He was easily influenced by his wife Alexandra, who was under the spell of Rasputin, a strange, shaggy, spiritualist from Siberia. Nicholas and Alexandra had a son who suffered from hemophilia, and great faith was put in Rasputin to keep the boy alive.

The Japanese destroyed three-quarters of the Russian
Navy and killed tens of thousands of soldiers in 1905

Although Rasputin was an illiterate, coarse peasant, usually drunk and dirty, he was a master of hypnotism. Alexandra took his advice on all matters, even firing trusted high-ranking officials on his word.

While all this was going on, Russia became an international disaster area. In 1905, the tiny nation of Japan dealt Russia a humiliating defeat in a border dispute. The Japanese destroyed three-quarters of the Russian navy and killed tens of thousands of soldiers.

Meanwhile in the streets of St. Petersburg, everyone began to doubt the sanity of Nicholas for taking the counsel of Rasputin. When people began to march in the streets demanding power and justice, Nicholas called their requests "senseless dreams." He could only accept the "power of God."

On January 22, 1905, a priest led 30,000 people to march on the czar's Winter Palace in St. Petersburg. They demanded lower taxes, better working conditions, and other reforms. Nicholas became frightened and fled the palace grounds before they arrived. The czar's cossacks fired guns into the crowd of peaceful demonstrators.

Blood ran through the palace square as five hundred people died and eight hundred more were wounded. The march was crushed on what became known as "Bloody Sunday," but the memory of that event would not pass quickly. Nicholas would pay dearly for "Bloody Sunday."

Czar Nicholas II, the last of the Romanov rulers

the roots of communism

**M**any revolutionary political parties in Russia took advantage of "Bloody Sunday" to further their goals. One of these groups called themselves Marxists, after Karl Marx, a German who lived in England. In 1848, Marx and his colleague Friedrich Engles wrote the *Communist Manifesto*. In that book, Marx predicted that a struggle would arise when the poor people battled the rich. Marx believed that the common working people of the world would unite against the bosses and the governments who used them as slaves and soldiers. When this happened, Marx wrote, there would be no more countries, only united workers, running the world together. Many people believed in Karl Marx's words when he said, "Workers of the world unite."

One of the early Marxist leaders was named Vladimir Ilyich Ulyanov, who changed his name to Lenin. Although Lenin was actually from the upper-classes, he used Marx's words to unite the Russian people.

Vladimir Lenin 1870-1924

Lenin was not a believer in Marxism, but it served his political ends to sing its praises.

Lenin called for a strike in 1905, causing Czar Nicholas to create a congress called a "Duma." Four congresses were elected over the next twelve years, each one canceling out the reforms of the other. As usual, chaos reigned. Lenin called for total revolution, but something even bigger intervened.

world war I

n 1914, the Archduke of Austria was murdered by a man from the small slavic country of Serbia. Russia sided with Serbia, so Austria declared war on Russia. Soon Germany, too, was fighting Russia. The fighting was quickly joined by France, England, and eventually, the United States. Blood drenched the countries of Europe while millions upon millions died in the fighting.

The Russian government was forced to fight on the battlefield and at home. The Russian people were much more concerned about their own well-being and showed little enthusiasm for the war effort. Only six weeks after the war began, Russian generals were already short of supplies and food. After drafting six million men, the government discovered it only had five million rifles.

In 1915, with the Russian army in full retreat and millions of men dead, Nicholas left St. Petersburg, on the advice of Rasputin, to take personal charge of the army. In his absence, Alexandra and Rasputin took control of the government.

Rasputin was a strange shaggy spiritualist from
Siberia who influenced Nicholas and Alexandra

rasputin's last gasp

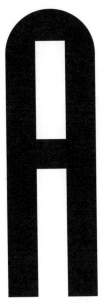

As Russian soldiers died, Russian hatred for the Germans increased. Fingers pointed to Rasputin and the German-born Alexandra. The German-sounding name of St. Petersburg was changed to Petrograd. Many people suspected Rasputin of being a German agent sent to destroy Russia.

At a palace party in December 1916, a group of Russian noblemen decided to do away with Rasputin. First, they poisoned his wine and cream cakes with cyanide. When that had no effect, they shot him. The injured Rasputin leapt off the floor and strangled his assailant. Finally, one of the assassins pumped bullets into Rasputin until he finally fell. To make sure he was dead, the noblemen dumped his body into the icy Neva River. That finally put an end to Rasputin's political career.

the falling czar

With Nicholas out of Petrograd and Rasputin dead, people began to take matters into their own hands. Trains to take soldiers to the front were in short supply as soldiers at the front commandeered them to desert by the thousands. When rioting broke out in Petrograd in March 1917, Nicholas ordered his troops to fire on the protesters. The soldiers mutinied. They joined the rioters, opened up the prisons, and set fire to police stations. Nicholas and his family were arrested and sent to Siberia, a fate he had ordered for countless others. A year later, the entire family was murdered, thus putting an end to over three hundred years of Romanov rule.

A new government was set up under socialist Alexander Kerensky. The government was rendered useless by in-fighting between intellectuals, landowners, peasants, and various radical groups. It was less able to govern than the czar.

the communists seize power

nto this power vacuum stepped Lenin who, with the backing of the workers and soldiers in Petrograd, directed a takeover. Lenin said, "History will not forgive us if we do not seize power now." First, Lenin's Bolshevik army ("Bolshevik" means "majority") occupied several train stations. Then they captured the State bank and the telephone exchanges, disconnecting government communications. By late afternoon, the Bolsheviks held all of Petrograd. The operation was carried out with few casualties.

Although the Bolsheviks had easily seized power in Petrograd, Moscow was captured only after a bitter struggle. Violent fighting raged between the 50,000-man Bolshevik Red Army and the 10,000-man Moscow City Council Army. By the end of November 1917, members of Lenin's Bolshevik party occupied all the important government buildings in Petrograd. They were Communists, and they had won the October Revolution. Lenin and the Communists were in.

Lenin realized that his first duty to his country was to ask the Germans for peace, however humiliating that might be. Russia was in no position to struggle on in a violent and senseless war. France, England and the United States, who were also fighting the Germans, were strongly opposed to Russia's peace treaty. Many wrongly suspected Lenin of being a German agent.

The Russian banks refused to recognize the Communist government. With the stroke of his pen, Lenin made the banks property of the state. He also decreed that the land belonged to those who worked on it, not the landlords. Next, he declared an eight-hour work day for the workers. The state took over almost every facet of business, enterprise, and manufacture. Unfortunately, the state lacked the experience and technical know-how to run all these businesses, adding even more chaos to an already overburdened system.

final word

For a time in 1918, Russia was swept with a unity that was unheard of in this staggering giant of a country. But everyone swept up in this unique upheaval was reduced to guesswork when it came time to get things done. Many guessed wrong.

The peasants had been delighted when they were told that the land belonged to those who worked it. In reality, the government began to confiscate the fruits of their labors to feed people in far away cities. At least before the revolution, landlords shared what little overstock there was with the local peasants. It seemed that nothing had changed.

Discontentment grew and counterrevolutionaries organized in many towns and cities. The Russian Imperial Army, left over from the days of the czar, reformed with crack soldiers fresh from the German front. They showed their superiority in several clashes with the Bolshevik army.

Dozens of different armies formed, each bent on overthrowing Lenin and the Communists. The United States even sent troops who occupied an area near the Arctic Circle for many months. It seemed that the workers of the world could not unite. The grim specter of a Russian civil war was about to become a grisly reality. While Lenin survived an assassination attempt, the people of Russia went to war with each other.

glossary

barbaric — Wild, primitive.

Boyar — The Russian upper class.

Communism — A system of government based on common ownership of property. In Soviet Communism all economic and social activity is controlled by a powerful central government.

Communist — A person who believes in Communism.

cossack — An elite group of soldiers from Southern Russia whose specialty was fighting on horseback. Organized as cavalry in the czarist army.

counterrevolutionary — Person who tries to start a revolution against a government that has just had a revolution.

czar — Title given to the king of Russia.

Duma — The main legislative assembly in Russia between 1905 and 1919. Created in 1905 by Czar Nicholas in order to slow revolutionary demands.

Nihilist — A nineteenth-century Russian party that used terrorism and assassination to promote reform.

Oprichnina — The dreaded secret police force first established in 1561 by Ivan the Terrible.

serf — A peasant. A person ruled by a Boyar.

Soviet Union — The common name used for the Union of Soviet Socialist Republics or USSR. Russia was renamed the USSR after the 1917 Communist revolution.

steppe — A vast, dry, treeless region with extreme temperature ranges usually found in southeastern Europe or Asia.

index

Alexander I- 29,30
Attila the Hun-9,10
Berlin Wall-4-8
Bloody Sunday-44,46
Catherine the Great-26,27,28
East Germany-6,7
Ivan the Terrible-18-21,40
Lenin, Vladimir-46,47,48,54-57
Marx, Karl-46
Napoleon-9,29,31
Nicholas II-40,43-45,48-50,52,53
Peter the Great-21-24,26
Rasputin-40,43,49,50,51,52
Romanov, Alexandra-40,43,49,50,51,53
Romanov, Anastasia-19,21,40
Serfs-15,16,19,28,32,34,36
Slavs-9,11,17
Vladimir I-11,12,15

FE